HEY, THAT'S
GRANDMA'S HOUSE!

Grandma's Message

Aura and Sol are both present at the family meeting

Succession planning is the topic that Uncle Ray is teaching

He will be in charge of making the family decisions

He knows how important it is for the next generation to carry out the vision

Recently, Aura and Sol lost their grandmother Lovie Ella and they are sad

They constantly think about the beautiful times that they all had

Like the time Lovie Ella said "Save, invest and buy assets"

And Always know the difference between good and bad debt

The Family Meeting

Grandma Lovie Ella left her home to the children and grandchildren

She wants them to keep the home and build an empire worth a billion

Aura and Sol believes they should respect grandma's wishes

But Aunt Sheena wants to sell the home to make quick riches

She said "We should sell the home, I could use the money"

She then snickered, but no one thought that it was funny

Aura and Sol's parents Mr. Dan and Mrs. Marcy stood in complete shock

Sol asked "Aunt Sheena, did you know real estate builds wealth just like stock?"

The Family Disagreement

Aunt Sheena is a little upset that Sol asked her that question

Uncle Ray interjected and said "Everyone have a seat, it's time for a lesson"

Uncle Ray asked "what is the most common vehicle used to build wealth"

Aunt Sheena sarcastically replied "cranes" and began to laugh at herself

This caused the rest of the family to laugh and that changed the mood

"Ding-Dong" goes the doorbell, the delivery man just in time with the food

Pure joy, as everyone begins to fix their plates and eat their meal

Uncle Ray received a phone call that he was clear to close on another deal

The Great News

Aura and Sol could hear the excitement in Uncle Ray's tone

So they patiently waited for Uncle Ray to hang up the phone

Aura asked "Uncle Ray what does it mean to get a clear to close?"

Uncle Ray replied "It means that you're approved to buy the home you chose"

Sol commented "Congratulations Unc, will you be living in that new home?"

Uncle Ray replied "Thanks Neph, no, its being rented, the renter will pay my loan"

Aura and Sol both smiled and said "That's cool, provide housing and get paid"

Uncle Ray replied "That's right, buy it and hold it, your wealth will never fade"

The Wealth Play

After hearing the great news everyone is happy for Uncle Ray

Uncle Ray went to the dry erase board and said "Check out this play"

Instead of selling grandma's home we should do a "cash-out re-fi"

Aunt Sheena yelled "Translation please" Uncle Ray said "hold-on, let me try"

We can pull some of the equity out and take on a new loan

This will give us money or capital to purchase a new home

We can rent out grandmas house to pay the new mortgage

Trust me when I say this "As a family, we can afford this"

The Nay Sayer

Aunt Sheena insisted "I don't think this will work, let's sell!"

Dad Dan looked at Mom Marcy as she said "If we sell then we fail"

Aunt Sheen replied "No, if we sell I get my money honey"

Uncle Ray interrupted "Wealth is having money on rainy days, not just the sunny"

Let's take a look at the bigger picture, and show some patience

We should be thinking long term goals, not instant gratification

Aura and Sol looked at Aunt Sheena and shook their head in disbelief

Sol whispered "She doesn't understand this is a turn of a new leaf"

The New Leaf

Aura and Sol went outside to get some fresh air

Aura look at Sol and said "I don't think Aunt Sheena is being fair"

A leaf fell from a tree and Sol picked it up

He turned and looked at Aura and said "This is us"

Aura seemed confused, Sol explained "At some point in life we all change

It may take Aunt Sheena a little longer, but she won't remain the same"

Interrupted by Aunt Sheena coming outside to say "Aura and Sol, I love you two

But as far as this house thing goes, I don't know what to do"

The Investor

Aunt Sheena checked the mail before going back into the house

She opened up a letter from an investor that created some doubts

The offer letter shows that it would easily give them a 6 figure return

But there were some things that Aunt Sheena needed to learn

Excited, Aunt Sheena showed Uncle Ray the investor offer letter

Uncle Ray said "Oh, that's nothing, I am sure that we can do much better"

Uncle Ray explained "The value of real estate will always rise

But holding onto your assets for as long as you can is the real prize

The Light Bulb

Uh-Oh, The light bulb in the hallway began to flicker

Aunt Sheena began staring at it, as she was stuck like a sticker

Mom Marcy and Dad Dan were walking by when they noticed the odd scene

Mom Marcy said "Sis, you look like a deer in the road looking at high beams"

Aunt Sheena laughed and she then asked "What is wrong with that light"

Mom Marcy laughingly replied "It's symbolic of how we look when we fight"

Dad Dan said "I will change the light bulb so that it can shine"

Sheena replied "So this is what it looks like when we use our mind"

The New Perspective

The family is in the gathering room talking about wealth

Uncle Ray said "Sometimes all we need is a different perspective to help"

Aunt Sheena replied "It's funny that I never thought about this before

I always thought that if you spend money it proves you aren't poor"

Sol and Aura rejoicingly shouted "I am so happy that we had this meeting

We were able to accomplish a gathering while grandma is no longer breathing"

Mom Marcy said "This is proof that grandma left a lasting impression

And we are doing her legacy justice by implementing one of her lessons"

The New Offer

A few days have passed and Aunt Sheena is checking the mail

It is another offer letter to see if they're willing to sell

This time it is from a real estate developer and he is offering more

Aunt Sheena thought about it, as the offer was quite an allure

She then called Uncle Ray on the phone to discuss the offer letter

Uncle Ray asked Aunt Sheena "will this offer change our lives forever"

Aunt Sheena replied "Probably not for everybody, so that means we'll decline"

Uncle Ray replied "You see now Sheena, I think you are starting to read my mind"

22 Oakwood drive
Jacksonville
Fl, 32214

14 April

Dear madam,

I am an investor in the area and I recently purchased
properties similar to yours.
I am looking to purchase a few more properties and I
believe that with your help I can achieve that goal.

I am ready and willing to make you a significant
offer for your home.

Yours sincerely

M.Bishop

The Final Decision

There is another family meeting to make the final decision

This is to be done with respect to Grandma's vision

At this particular meeting, the family lawyer is present

He is assisting with estate planning, so that everyone remains pleasant

Estate planning offers protection for the things and people we love

This allows everyone to feel at peace and not have to push and shove

Mom Marcy exclaimed "We will hold onto this property forever, if we must"

The family lawyer replied "Then you all should put it into a trust"

The Wealth

Confused, Sol asked the family lawyer "What is a Trust"

He replied "Think of it like a pizza, it's there to protect your cheese like crust

A trust will ensure that everything you worked for is not easily taken away"

Sol turned to smile at Uncle Ray and said "I guess this house is here to stay"

Aunt Sheena shouted out "This is excellent I would really like this protection"

Mom Marcy replied "See girl I told you Ray always steers us in the right direction"

Aura and Sol are really excited that the family has no more doubts

They began to dance and repeatedly shout "Hey, That's Grandma's House"

COLORING PAGE

COLORING PAGE

COLORING PAGE

Made in the USA
Columbia, SC
28 December 2023